Floppy Did This!

Written by Roderick Hunt
Illustrated by Alex Brychta

Chip did this.

It is Biff.

Biff did this.

It is Kipper.

Kipper did this.

It is Mum.

Oh, no!

Floppy did this!

Talk about the story

Spot the difference

Find the five differences in the two pictures of Kipper.

Who Is It?

Written by Roderick Hunt
Illustrated by Alex Brychta

Who is it?

It is Kipper.

Who is it?

It is Biff.

Who is it?

It is Chip.

Is it Kipper?

No. It is Floppy!

Talk about the story

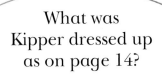
What was Kipper dressed up as on page 14?

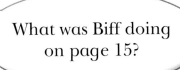
What was Biff doing on page 15?

What was the trick on page 19?

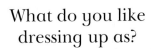
What do you like dressing up as?

Twins

Find the twin clowns.

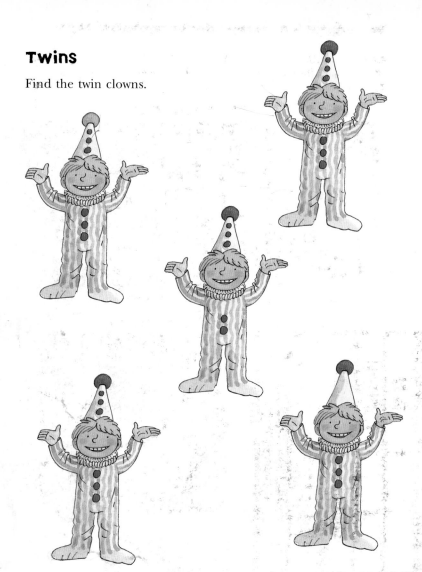